TRENDS IN SOUTHEAST ASIA

The **ISEAS – Yusof Ishak Institute** (formerly Institute of Southeast Asian Studies) is an autonomous organization established in 1968. It is a regional centre dedicated to the study of socio-political, security, and economic trends and developments in Southeast Asia and its wider geostrategic and economic environment. The Institute's research programmes are grouped under Regional Economic Studies (RES), Regional Strategic and Political Studies (RSPS), and Regional Social and Cultural Studies (RSCS). The Institute is also home to the ASEAN Studies Centre (ASC), the Singapore APEC Study Centre and the Temasek History Research Centre (THRC).

ISEAS Publishing, an established academic press, has issued more than 2,000 books and journals. It is the largest scholarly publisher of research about Southeast Asia from within the region. ISEAS Publishing works with many other academic and trade publishers and distributors to disseminate important research and analyses from and about Southeast Asia to the rest of the world.

THE MILITARY IN BURMA/MYANMAR

On the Longevity of Tatmadaw Rule and Influence

David I. Steinberg

ISSUE

6

2021

 YUSOF ISHAK
INSTITUTE

Published by: ISEAS Publishing
                 30 Heng Mui Keng Terrace
                 Singapore 119614
                 publish@iseas.edu.sg
                 http://bookshop.iseas.edu.sg

ISEAS Library Cataloguing-in-Publication Data

Name(s): Steinberg, David I., 1928-, author.
Title: The military in Burma/Myanmar : on the longevity of Tatmadaw rule and influence / David I. Steinberg.
Description: Singapore : ISEAS – Yusof Ishak Institute, May 2021. | Series: Trends in Southeast Asia, ISSN 0219-3213 ; TRS6/21 | Includes bibliographical references.
Identifiers: ISBN 9789814951715 (soft cover) | ISBN 9789814951722 (pdf)
Subjects: LCSH: Myanmar—Armed forces—Political activity. | Myanmar—Politics and government.
Classification: LCC DS501 I59T no. 6(2021)

Typeset by Superskill Graphics Pte Ltd
Printed in Singapore by Markono Print Media Pte Ltd

FOREWORD

The economic, political, strategic and cultural dynamism in Southeast Asia has gained added relevance in recent years with the spectacular rise of giant economies in East and South Asia. This has drawn greater attention to the region and to the enhanced role it now plays in international relations and global economics.

The sustained effort made by Southeast Asian nations since 1967 towards a peaceful and gradual integration of their economies has had indubitable success, and perhaps as a consequence of this, most of these countries are undergoing deep political and social changes domestically and are constructing innovative solutions to meet new international challenges. Big Power tensions continue to be played out in the neighbourhood despite the tradition of neutrality exercised by the Association of Southeast Asian Nations (ASEAN).

The **Trends in Southeast Asia** series acts as a platform for serious analyses by selected authors who are experts in their fields. It is aimed at encouraging policymakers and scholars to contemplate the diversity and dynamism of this exciting region.

THE EDITORS

Series Chairman:
 Choi Shing Kwok

Series Editor:
 Ooi Kee Beng

Editorial Committee:
 Daljit Singh
 Francis E. Hutchinson
 Norshahril Saat

The Military in Burma/Myanmar: On the Longevity of Tatmadaw Rule and Influence

By David I. Steinberg

EXECUTIVE SUMMARY

- The Myanmar military has dominated that complex country for most of the period since independence in 1948. The fourth coup of 1 February 2021 was the latest by the military to control those aspects of society it deemed essential to its own interests, and its perception of state interests.
- The military's institutional power was variously maintained by rule by decree, through political parties it founded and controlled, and through constitutional provisions it wrote that could not be amended without its approval.
- This fourth coup seems a product of personal demands for power between Senior General Min Aung Hlaing and Aung San Suu Kyi, and the especially humiliating defeat of the military-backed party at the hands of the National League for Democracy in the November 2020 elections.
- The violent and bloody suppression of widespread demonstrations continues, compromise seems unlikely, and the previous diarchic governance will not return.
- Myanmar's political and economic future is endangered and suppression will only result in future outbreaks of political frustration.

The Military in Burma/Myanmar: On the Longevity of Tatmadaw Rule and Influence

By David I. Steinberg[1]

OVERVIEW[2]

Burma was "quite unlike any land you know about," so Kipling wrote. He thought it unique even if appended to India as a province. But he could not have predicted the future singular role of the military in that country, for the Tatmadaw has been, and remains, the longest-ruling military elite in modern Asia, and perhaps in the contemporary world. For over half a century it commanded power, ran the state, and has been pivotal since independence in 1948. Its dominance lay not only in its complete control over the powers of state coercion, but also in its early prestige and heritage, and, later, its vice-like grip on all important elements of the society.

Its militarized Burman leadership was the only Asian group that fought early against the Allies for independence early in World War II, despite very limited military training those participating received from their Japanese allies and before the Burmese (mostly Burmans) turned against the Axis in March 1945. Unusual in Asia, the military formed

[1] David I. Steinberg is distinguished professor of Asian studies emeritus, Georgetown University.

[2] This essay will use Burma as the name of the state before 1989, and Myanmar thereafter, but Burmese for the language, all citizens, and as an adjective. Tatmadaw is often used for the Burmese military. Burman (Bamar) refers to the majority ruling ethnic group. The author thanks those who commented on earlier drafts for their help, but the responsibility for sins of commission or omission is the author's alone.

political parties; this became a pattern.[3] Its leader, Aung San, orchestrated a conference at Panglong in 1947 that brought some minorities into what became the Union of Burma. He negotiated independence from Great Britain in 1948, and his assassination just before its fruition gave an almost mystic reverence to him, his family, and those military personnel associated with him. The Tatmadaw saved the state from multiple communist and ethnic rebellions in the 1950s, tried (unsuccessfully) to counter fleeing Nationalist Chinese anti-communist remnants that occupied some of Burma's northern reaches, and later, on multiple occasions, prevented actual and perceived threats of secession and what it continuously referred to as internal "chaos". In 1958, it unfortunately acquired both false confidence in its capacity to govern and to manage an economy as well as in the widespread, inevitable corruption of its civilian elite.

This leadership was early viewed, and viewed themselves, as patriots and defenders of the state, and the Tatmadaw was a most desirable career, the officer class graduating from the Defence Services Academy at Maymyo with University of Rangoon degrees, although they were too junior to become leaders of the 1962 coup.[4] But the ineptness of its control after the coup of 1962 became evident as the rigidity of its authority increased, its intent of perpetual power became more evident, its fostering of whimsical policies and ideological rigidity proliferated, and authoritarian rule spread. Its odious influence was compounded by the extreme personalization of power—a traditional and continuing aspect of Burmese authority. It claimed to be the state's guardian from external dangers but, most importantly, from multiple examples of internal "chaos", though such disturbances were often created by its own mistaken policies. The Tatmadaw's three earlier coups, and that of 1 February 2021, the fourth, with its mandated constitutional provisions,

---

[3] The first was the Anti-Fascist People's Freedom League in 1946, then the Burma Socialist Programme Party (BSPP), then the National Unity Party (NUF), and later the Union Solidarity and Development Party (USDP).

[4] Of the nineteen members of the SLORC in 1988, three were from the initial Academy graduating class.

exemplify and illustrate the extent of its control and intent. Its influence today continues to be profound if not popular. More muted until February 2021, its aspirations for a political role remain and are blatantly proclaimed and solidified in institutional and constitutional provisions as well as, once again, with troops in the streets. Understanding its history, its position and these aspirations is essential to comprehending the contemporary dynamics of Myanmar.

Yet an interpretation of the complexities of Myanmar as the conflict between autocratic and democratic rule is both simplistic and misleading. This aspect is but one of the multiple prisms through which the contemporary history of that state should be examined. These include competing political parties, a major generational gap between the older Tatmadaw leadership and the Z generation more exposed to international trends, between conflicting personalized leadership, between ethnic majority and minority tensions as evidenced in a variety of institutional settings, and (although often ignored) between traditional and culturally dominant attitudes towards authority and power and those emanating from transitional concepts of governance. Myanmar's uniqueness lies both in its history and in its contemporary and explosive intricacies.

THE CREATION OF THE STATE AND ITS PROTECTION (1948–58)

The room, a virtual shrine, in the Secretariat Building in which on 19 July 1947, Bogyoke (General) Aung San and his colleagues, the presumptive cabinet of what was to be the newly independent Union of Burma on 4 January 1948, were assassinated, remains—restored as a tribute to his leadership. That date is commemorated as Azarni (Martyr's) Day and is the most solemn in the country's calendar.[5] The date, 12 February 1947,

---

[5] Three national commemorative days are directly associated with Aung San: 12 February (Union Day), 27 March (Armed Forces Day—also called Resistance Day, when the Burmese turned against the British in World War II), and 19 July, the day of his assassination. The only other non-religious holiday is New Year's Day.

on which he brought together diverse ethnic groups to a conference at Panglong in the Shan State to convince them to join in an independent national union is still celebrated as Union Day. He negotiated independence from Great Britain in London. His memory is constantly revived, his pictures ubiquitous; his wife was appointed as ambassador to India, and his daughter, Aung San Suu Kyi, the civilian leader of a "quasi-civilian" state after many years of military-imposed house arrest, during which time the military purposely and vigorously diminished his memory to lessen his daughter's familial claim to legitimacy.[6] It has been extensively revived.

After World War II, some in the British government wanted Aung San tried for the murder of a Karen chief or as a traitor, as he organized a Burmese contingent that supported the Japanese invasion of Burma, only turning against the Japanese in March 1945 on the cusp of war's end. Provided with the title of Bogyoke (general), he had received no formal military training—similar to his colleague, General (also Bogyoke) Ne Win, who became leader of the Burma army in 1949, sometime deputy prime minister in the 1950s civilian era, and after 1962, until his retirement in 1988, variously president, senior general, and chairman of the single-party state that Burma had become—the dictator of an autocratic, military-ruled government.

"The Burma army on the eve of World War II was more an embodiment of British colonial attitudes than of Burmese reality."[7] Only 12.3 per cent were ethnically Burman (Bamar), as the British recruited from the hill tribes on their Indian model. Aung San founded the Burma Independence Army, which was replaced by the Burma National Army under Japanese titular-sponsored "independence". This army numbered 20,000 to 30,000 troops when the Burmese turned against the Japanese on 27 March 1945.

---

[6] Aung San's image was removed from currency notes in 1988, and only restored after 2016. It was also removed from postage stamps and only reinstituted by Aung San Suu Kyi.

[7] David I. Steinberg, *Burma's Road Toward Development: Growth and Ideology under Military Rule* (Boulder, CO: Westview Press, 1981), p. 12. The British did not recruit Burmans until the 1930s, as that ethnic majority had revolted against British rule.

On independence, the Burmese military was headed by a Karen, General Smith Dun, who had trained in India.[8] This was a sop to the Karen ethnic group who had long wanted an independent state for their adherents. Smith Dun was loyal to the regime, which nevertheless replaced him with a Burman, General Ne Win. The Tatmadaw was small, about 110,000, and although the military planners in the mid-1950s wanted an expansion of two armoured and one infantry divisions to hold off a potential Chinese invasion (the only likely foreign enemy) until the United States came to their rescue—the Korean War model. U Nu decided it was too expensive and that Chinese friendship was a better course.[9]

The decade from the independence of the country to the "constitutional coup" that ended the first period of civilian rule was tumultuous. Two communist rebellions were active and a danger to the democratic socialist state, the Karen minority was in revolt and briefly occupied some suburbs of the capital, and various *tat* (armed private militias) controlled some local districts. Remnant Chinese Nationalist (Kuomintang) forces, defeated by the Chinese Communist People's Liberation Army, fled into northern Burma where they were preparing anti-communist movements on the mainland and were covertly assisted by both Taiwan and the United States. Prime Minister U Nu feared the People's Liberation Army would engage them and occupy parts of northern Burma, which China had long claimed since before the twentieth century. When the media wrote about a Rangoon government, for a period that was almost literally true.

The Tatmadaw was an important avenue for social mobility and a desirable career. In a society with strong civilian political divisions, personal animosities and power bases, corruption, and a stumbling economy, the military's apparent cohesion and administrative capacity was admired. The civilian inept handling of both the administration

---

[8] General Smith Dun. See his autobiography *Memoirs of the Four-Foot Colonel* (Cornell University Southeast Asia Data Papers #113, 1980).

[9] Brigadier Maung Maung, chief of military planning and the third highest ranking officer. Personal communication.

and the economy greatly distressed General Ne Win, who was clearly powerful even under civilian rule and held deputy prime minister responsibilities in 1949.

THE "CONSTITUTIONAL COUP", THE CARETAKER GOVERNMENT (1958–60), AND CIVILIAN AFTERMATH

Elections were to take place in 1958, but the Anti-Fascist People's Freedom League, the large umbrella and dominant political party with over 1.3 million members, had split into personalized factions even though ideologically most were socialists. The military were disturbed by Prime Minister U Nu's pardon of leftist soldiers who had formed a political party. U Nu only survived a no-confidence vote in Parliament through their support of the extreme left National United Front, which the military suspected as being proto-communist. The Front wanted to be incorporated into the military, against the judgment of General Ne Win. Civil war fears loomed.

Senior military personnel approached the prime minister suggesting that he allow the military to take over for a period (initially six months that was extended to about eighteen months) to avoid internal conflict. The legislature agreed; it was characterized as a "coup by consent" or a "pseudo-constitutional-peaceful-military *coup d'état*".[10] "U Nu took the constitutional way out and Ne Win the constitutional way in."[11]

The objectives of the military, which ruled by decree, were to establish law and order, eliminate economic "insurgents" (clearly aimed at foreigners), and prepare for elections, which were eventually held in 1960. This was a successful period even if reflecting its authoritarian rule. The "caretaker" military forcibly lowered prices in the bazaars,

---

[10] Dr Baw Maw (former dictator under the Japanese-sponsored wartime government) and William Johnstone, respectively. Quoted in Steinberg, *Burma's Road Toward Development*, p. 16.

[11] Sein Win, *The Split Story*, quoted in Steinberg, *Burma's Road Toward Development*, p. 91.

removed over 160,000 illegal squatters from downtown Rangoon to the rice paddies of the suburbs (the military repeated this in 1988/89), diminished insurgent control, negotiated the Chinese border agreement (signed later by U Nu), eliminated the legal authority of the hereditary ethnic Shan and Kayah leaders, and passed a universal (male-female) military conscription law passed (but never enforced) on an Israeli model.

The military then was uncorrupted, and instituted a vigorous, effective administration over that short time. But the efficacy of its rule then prompted ill-considered self-confidence in their capacity to govern more extensively and over long periods. The Tatmadaw occupied parts of the Shan State, which it administered in lieu of civilian authorities in those regions.[12] Importantly, it expanded the Defence Services Institute, which had begun years before as a type of military Post Exchange or cooperative, into an extensive economic behemoth of thirteen separate military-run enterprises encompassing such businesses as an international shipping line, a department store, banking, hotels, trading, and other fields.[13] This served as the first instance of a continuing Tatmadaw effort to control significant elements of the economy. In 1959, the military published its "National Ideology and the Role of the Defence Services". The priorities were nothing new: rule of law, democracy, and socialism.[14] Their inflated confidence was reflected in the volume the military produced on its administration—the picture on the dustcover of Hercules cleaning out the Augean stables.[15] The Tatmadaw seemed to believe that vigour, esprit and a strong command system could replace sector competence.

The elections in 1960, held under military auspices, were reasonably fair. The military-favoured party lost to U Nu, who inaugurated a

[12] See Mary P. Callahan, *Making Enemies. War and State Building in Myanmar* (Ithaca, NY: Cornell University Press, 2003).

[13] See Steinberg, *Burma's Road Toward Development*, p. 17.

[14] See Yoshihiro Nakanishi, *Strong Soldiers, Failed Revolution. The State and the Military in Burma, 1962–88* (Singapore and Kyoto: National University of Singapore Press, 2003), p. 174.

[15] Director of Information, *Is Trust Vindicated? A Chronicle of Trust, Striving, and Triumph. Being an Account of the Accomplishments of the Government of the Union of Burma*, 12 November 1958 – 1 February 1960. Rangoon, 1960.

short-lived government that was inept, illustrated by his advocacy of constructing 60,000 sand pagodas to solve the state's problems. More importantly for its immediate effect, he campaigned, and later made good his promise, by making Buddhism the state religion, thereby causing the Kachin, an important element of the military, to go into revolt against the government. General Ne Win adamantly opposed that move by U Nu, which intensified the ethnic rebellions, as many in the military and some of the minorities were heavily Christian.

The first decade and a half of independence illustrated to the Tatmadaw the self-seeking incompetence of civilian politicians who lacked both vision and resolution of the state's problems, and thus could not be trusted with national administration. That attitude set the stage for the military's self-derived need for the perpetuation of its role in the national administration.

THE BURMA SOCIALIST PROGRAMME PARTY AND ITS COLLAPSE (1962–88)

The Tatmadaw's primary articulated focus has been the preservation of the state—the Union of Burma, and its later renamed designations. The means of support to the concept has varied, but its continued focus has never been in doubt. Yet the national concept of a "union" has been lacking. There has been no overarching national consensus of what it means to be a citizen of the country. It has been a state, but not, emotionally, a nation.[16] Ethnic minorities, some one-third of the total population, have often called for secession from the Union by force of armed insurrection or later demanded some form of autonomous federal structure, promised by Aung San at the Panglong Conference but never actually implemented. Burma from its inauguration has been effectively a unitary state controlled by a Burman Buddhist majority population.

---

[16] See David I. Steinberg, "The Problem of Democracy in the Republic of the Union of Myanmar: Neither Nation-State nor State-Nation?", in *Southeast Asian Affairs 2012*, edited by Daljit Singh and Pushpa Thambipillai (Singapore: Institute of Southeast Asian Studies, 2012).

The second *coup d'état*, one that was without civilian consent, was ostensibly to preserve the Union. The Burmese constitution of 1947 stipulated that the Shan and Kayah States could opt out of the national union after ten years and with a referendum, but no central government was likely to allow that to happen. The Shan leaders nevertheless met in Rangoon and there was talk that U Nu might grant them more autonomy. General Ne Win had regarded any form of federalism as the first stage to secession. This was the excuse for the coup on 2 March 1962, the arrest of all civilian leaders, and the eventual dissolution of civilian institutions associated with the previous administration. One death resulted, when security personnel shot and killed the son of President Sao Shwe Taik, who was of the Shan nobility. Some believe that this fear of secession was merely the excuse and that the maladministration of, frustration with, and disdain for incompetent civilian rule would have resulted in a military takeover in any case.[17]

A seventeen-person military council controlled everything, including forming the Burma Socialist Programme Party (BSPP) with initially and entirely a cadre of high-ranking officers. Since its early days, it published the "Burmese Sway to Socialism", the BSPP charter, and somewhat later "The System of Correlation of Man and His Environment", the pseudo- philosophical basis of the regime. This was a uniquely Burmese socialist agenda. Dr Ba Maw remarked, "It is also Burmese; it wants socialism, which is good, but it wants it in a Burmese form and in a Burmese way, which is better still."[18] Over the next couple of years, all other political parties were banned, censorship imposed, student protests violently suppressed, the judicial system destroyed, the bureaucracy purged of senior officials, foreigners (especially Indians—those from the subcontinent—and Chinese) expelled, and a nationalization of all

---

[17] One should note that in the Western social science literature of the period, there were articles that the military was the hope for development in the Third World because they were generally focused, disciplined and task-oriented, in contrast to amorphous, self-serving civilian leaderships. In that period of the Cold War, such militaries were anti-communist, which may have affected this judgment.

[18] *Nation* (Rangoon), 2 May 1962. See Fred von der Mehden, "The Burmese Way to Socialism", *Asian Survey* 3, no. 3 (March 1963): 129–35.

industry begun. Buddhist monks were finally registered, and in 1982 a highly nationalistic citizenship law was enacted. To run a socialist government requires a talented bureaucracy, but it had been decimated. Eminent Burmese economists left the country.[19]

Over time, some 15,000 large and small businesses were nationalized, and military officers, often quite junior ones, had positions of authority at local levels. While cooperatives were encouraged, land generally remained in private hands, although since the 1947 constitution the state was the legal owner of all land in the country. By 1965, the BSPP (also called the Lanzin Party) had expanded, but the leadership was still only twenty military officers, while an additional 99,000 were "candidate" members (29 per cent from the Tatmadaw and 1.2 per cent from the police), and 167,000 "sympathizers". By 1971, it was 58 per cent military, and two-thirds of the Tatmadaw were either full or associate members. To rise in the bureaucracy effectively required membership in the party. Indoctrination was essential. The Central School of Political Science was established in 1963 (upgraded to an Institute in 1971) and in the first decade trained over 29,000 cadres, while the Tatmadaw set up Command Services Training Courses through the party and trained over 15,000 militarymen. It was clearly ideology over pragmatism. The bureaucracy had been purged of the civilian elites of the previous administration, including the prestigious Burma Civil Service that had evolved out of the Indian Civil Service.

It was evident at that time that this was not to be a temporary imposition of military rule. The intent clearly was to develop a militarily controlled political system into the indefinite future. From the outset, the BSPP was completely military-dominated and controlled, and it was stipulated that one could never resign from the party. The BSPP

---

[19] It is significant that when Park Chung Hee conducted his coup in Korea in 1961, he recognized that his military leaders knew little about economics, and he planned to force back to Korea overseas Korean PhD holders in economics. The United States convinced him this was not a good idea, but better to entice them back. So the Korea Development Institute was formed to develop policies. It was an obvious success.

gradually expanded, but it still was essentially military in composition and completely in leadership. By 1971, the military had increased the BSPP sufficiently to hold its first party congress, a first step towards its development of a new constitution. It changed policy emphasis to agriculture from an industrial proletariat that was essentially lacking. This new constitution was inaugurated in 1974 and stipulated that this was a single-party socialist state run by the BSPP, along the lines of the Eastern European models of that period.

Ne Win was in command as virtual dictator. His control was not only because of his titular roles over the period—president, party chair—but also because he controlled all significant promotions within the military and filled positions with those who were part of his entourage (including non-officers)—one dating to his command of the Fourth Burma Rifles in the 1940s.[20] From 1972 to 1988, the military transferred 1,743 officers to the civilian administration; 43.6 per cent were to People's Councils.[21]

The military didn't understand what they didn't know and thought that enthusiasm, esprit, and the command structure could replace sector competence.[22] Ideological conformity in recruitment of military elites was evident. But ideology was always subject to Ne Win's unsound policy whims. It was not only the expulsion of foreigners who had a singular hold on the economy at many levels, but demonetizations, change in currency notes so they would add up to 90, the astrological

---

[20] Ne Win's authority extended even to the early 1990s; when General Saw Maung (1988–92) was ousted because of growing mental issues, Ne Win was first consulted by the examining physician to approve his dismissal. Personal communication. Among those prominent from that unit were Brigadier Aung Gyi, Brigadier Tin Pe, General Kyaw Htin (Chief of Staff, later BSPP General Secretary), Lt. Gen. Aye Ko (Vice Chief of Staff, later Vice President BSPP), Lt. Gen. Tun Yi (Vice Chief of Staff and later Chair, National Unity Party), Brig. General Sein Lwin (later short-term president), and President Saw Maung. Vice President San Yu was in the Third Burma Rifles.

[21] Nakanishi, *Strong Soldiers, Failed Revolution*, p. 161.

[22] D. Steinberg, "Anomalies: The Republic of Korea and the Republic of the Union of Myanmar Economic Development and the Roles of the Military", unpublished paper.

number that would ensure Ne Win lived to be 90 (it was "successful", as he died at 92), altering traffic patterns from left-hand drive to the right, and his mercurial whims and leadership.[23]

Although Ne Win's control over promotions gave him unprecedented authority, he was once challenged by some officers in 1976 (quickly suppressed) as it became evident that the economy was in widespread decline.[24] The black market dominated retail trade, corruption flourished, and the state economic enterprises, those run directly by the government, were economic drains on limited resources. Yet the administration felt it could not reform these state enterprises, which had become major and redundant avenues of employment, for it was warned by local officials that if jobs were eliminated, social unrest would spread.[25]

There was a growing but unarticulated split between active-duty military and BSPP military as the economic situation deteriorated (pre-war living standards were only reached in 1976), and this also became apparent when the military did not advocate victory for the reconstituted BSPP (the National Unity Party) in the ignored 1990 elections. If an active-duty officer were transferred to the BSPP, it was the end of his military promotion channel. Active-duty officers looked down on the BSPP economic performance.

Economic mismanagement continued and the economy deteriorated; import costs rose, prompting another crisis. In September 1987, the military denationalized rice and grain trade but also demonetized all

---

[23] When the author officially explored USAID reentry into the country in 1979, he was warned by members of the cabinet that projects would require Ne Win's personal approval, and the cabinet would decide when his irascible mood was appropriate for such approval. The US fiscal year was irrelevant.

[24] Former Singapore Prime Minister Lee Kuan Yew said that when he played golf with Ne Win, he was accompanied by a squad of troops, indicating his concerns. Personal communication, 2007.

[25] Reforms were theoretically built into the system, however. Single-party parliamentary representatives were to go back to their home districts, listen to complaints, and then correct problems. A cabinet colonel explained that it did not work, as people did not complain. Personal communication.

Burmese currency notes over the equivalent of US$2.50 in value. In December of that year, the UN declared that Burma was one the world's least developed nations (the government withheld this information from the public until April 1988, but had lobbied for it to lower international interest rates). This degradation was especially profound, as on independence many predicted Burma would be the most developed state in the region.

Political and economic frustrations were evident, and in March 1988 an apolitical student dispute was brutally stopped by riot police, igniting what became a people's revolution. Additional state atrocities became widely apparent even in a society where information was strictly controlled.[26] Schools were closed, riots were widespread and, from a Tatmadaw vantage point, "chaos" reigned. As the Tatmadaw violently suppressed rioting and looting, many students fled government control to rebel border areas and Thailand. Some 3,000 people are now estimated to have been killed in the demonstrations and the follow-up to the resulting coup, although an earlier estimate was 10,000. This was a failed people's revolution—a social upheaval.

In July 1988, during this ferment, the BSPP held its convention. Ne Win asked whether the party would agree to change into a multi-party system. It demurred. Ne Win, despite the prohibition against resigning, did so, taking with him his sycophantic President General San Yu. The party elected General Sein Lwin, detested by the public for his brutal suppression of demonstrators, Sein Lwin's rule lasted but about two weeks, to be replaced by that of Dr Maung Maung, the sole civilian (and another sycophant) Ne Win had trusted. He promised multi-party elections but this could not suppress discontent.

---

[26] Forty-one students and others were smothered to death in a van after they had been arrested. The administration publicly denied this, but Ne Win, who was abroad, returned, and he entered the room of his cabinet, his hand shaking as he held a paper in it, and asked if this were true. The cabinet admitted it was, and Ne Win was fearful of more public uprisings. Personal communication from a participant.

THE JUNTA AND THEIN SEIN ADMINISTRATION (1988–2016)

On 18 September 1988, the Tatmadaw instituted the third coup against, but actually in favour of, the former Tatmadaw leaders. It was an attempt to prop up military rule, and it succeeded, but at great cost to the people. It seemed evident at that time that the Tatmadaw intended their authority to continue and last in some form.[27]

The new leaders, led by General Saw Maung (1988–92, when he became unhinged and thought himself the reincarnation of one of the Burmese kings), formed a junta called the State Law and Order Restoration Council (SLORC). It quickly formulated new policies, including abandonment of state socialism (but not dirigiste policies), and promised multi-party elections. Controls were reinforced on information, but party formation was allowed to proceed, and eventually some ninety-three separate parties registered for the May 1990 elections. The most significant of these parties was the National League for Democracy (NLD), led by Aung Gyi, the former second officer under Ne Win in the 1950s and others formerly in the military. Aung San Suu Kyi was in the country, and because of her heritage was appointed as secretary (she was deemed too young to lead the elder prominent leaders). Her early prominence and popularity became apparent at her speech at the Shwedagon Pagoda on 26 August 1988. Her speech, in which she appealed to the Tatmadaw to become a force in which the people could place their trust and reliance, infuriated the SLORC. She was placed under house arrest in 1989, a condition that (with some on-off restrictions) lasted for

---

[27] Senior officials in the new administration told the author this in 1988. As former Minister of Information U Ye Htut noted, "Senior General Than Shwe had nurtured the Union Solidarity and Development Association since 1993. His intention was to establish a political force that had the same political ideologies as the Tatmadaw so that a political force would represent the military after the Tatmadaw withdrew from politics step by step." Interview, "Will Myanmar's Military Sever Its Relationship With the Union Solidarity and Development Party?", *The Irrawaddy*, 28 November 2020. The USDA became a political party later—the USDP.

close to sixteen years while her popularity, even cult status, grew. While she continuously spoke of her respect for the Tatmadaw, which she often reminded everyone that her father had founded, it remained gravely suspicious of her.

The resulting May 1990 elections have generally been regarded as relatively free and fair. The NLD won a sweeping majority of some 82 per cent of the seats with about 59 per cent of the vote. The military-backed National Unity Party did poorly. Whether this was a vote in favour of democracy or whether it was prompted by widespread dissatisfaction with the military in administration, or both, is still conjecture. But the question was: What was this election for? A new government? A body to write a new constitution after which elections would again take place? Opinions differ, and the SLORC was responsible for the confusion. The SLORC nullified the election outcome under patently absurd excuses. Order 1/90 issued on 27 July 1990 declared that only the junta "has the legislative power", and that "representatives elected by the people" would merely be responsible for drafting a new constitution for a future democratic state."

The NLD maintained that the election was for a new government, which thus had political legitimacy, and power should forthwith be turned over to it.[28] The NLD spokesman promised there would be no "Nuremberg trials" (responsibility for previous crimes), a comment that while designed to reassure the Tatmadaw had the reverse effect (such a provision was included in the 2008 constitution).

By 1992, the SLORC's control was virtually absolute, and with it the rise in prominence of Military Intelligence (officially, the Directorate of Defence Services Intelligence), headed by General Khin Nyunt, who was Secretary-1 of the SLORC, which changed its name to the State Peace and Development Council (SPDC) in 1997, indicating its new focus. Khin Nyunt led a series of negotiations with several ethnic armed groups, resulting in mostly verbal ceasefires. This was a highly nationalistic period with the change in colonial-era names (from streets and cities to

---

[28] The United States and much of the West supported this position, which was, in effect, "regime change" to which the military would not agree.

that of the country) and an emphasis on mistrust of foreigners, who, it was argued, could not love the country (i.e., Aung San Suu Kyi's marriage to an English academic), while trying to attract foreign investment, and opening the country to tourists (beyond 24-hour or week-long stopovers) for the first time since 1962.

In 1993, the Tatmadaw instituted a highly selective and heavily scripted isolated constitutional convention, the purpose of which was to produce a legal document (the third since independence, and the second to solidify its control) that would articulate and ensure the Tatmadaw's essential power interests and those it felt critical for the state. In addition to an explicit reference to the Tatmadaw's political role in state affairs, it provided military veto power over constitutional changes by ensuring amendments could not be passed without its approval through allocation of active-duty military to 25 per cent of all seats at all levels and ensured that critical ministries remain in military hands (Defence, Home Affairs, Border Affairs), that at least one vice president would be from the military, and that the National Defence and Security Council have a majority military presence. The presidency or vice presidencies could not be held by anyone with close foreign citizenship (effectively eliminating Aung San Suu Kyi but also some Tatmadaw officers). A manipulated confirming referendum, which the United States surreptitiously attempted to undercut, was held in May 2008,[29] perhaps quickly imposed by the disconcerting *sangha* demonstrations against the military (mistakenly in the West called the "saffron revolution") in 2007 that made them

---

[29] This was held in the wake of cyclone Nargis, which killed some 138,000 people, but to change the date (important dates were determined by appropriate astrological calculations to ensure success) would have been to threaten its karmic rewards. Natural disasters are indications of the loss of legitimacy— positive karma. "the 2008 Constitution needs to be understood, i.e., as a desperate attempt by the military to stabilize its power at the very moment they had lost their mandate as legitimate representatives of the moral karmic order. The claim, in 2008 as today [2021] that they alone can grant or revoke democratic civilian power-sharing is as much a statement about the de facto truth of ongoing military might as an assertion of the karmic legitimacy." Ingrid Jordt, "Notes on the Coup in Myanmar: Karmic Kingship, Legitimacy, and Sovereignty", *Contending Modernities*, 6 April 2021.

concerned over continuing, unpopular direct rule. In November 2010, new clearly controlled elections, which the NLD boycotted, resulted in the inauguration of the moderate Thein Sein (general, former prime minister) government in 2011 under the auspices of the Union Solidarity and Development Party (USDP), an offshoot of a supposedly military-controlled civil society group that in 1993 had about 38 per cent of the total population as members. Many of the civilian elected leaders were also retired military, as they were often the most prominent and best educated in some local populations.

During the SPDC period, however, military control over the now "unsocialist" economy was advanced through the formation of the Union of Myanmar Economic Holdings Corporation (1990)[30] and the Myanmar Economic Corporation (1997), both directly under military control but incorporated separately from state-sponsored enterprises. These large organizations, probably the largest non-state businesses in the country, with ventures into a multitude of fields, employed tens of thousands of workers and had major foreign investment agreements. As the economy opened, foreign investment laws were passed, and retired military and civilians had access to economic opportunities—some legal and many designed for "cronies."[31]

The complete control over the avenues of social mobility and civil society was relaxed, education opened, the press and media given restricted rights, public demonstrations allowed with advance approval, and some criticisms of state policies and actions permitted. Legitimacy was still sought through extensive promotion of Buddhist rituals, and a distinct nationalistic, and increasingly anti-Islamic, agenda became apparent.

---

[30] This was incorporated in 1990 with a potential capital of 20 per cent of 1991 GNP, and a working capital of K40 million. The Ministry of Defence Directorate of Procurement held 40 per cent of its assets, and the other 60 per cent were divided among military units, and active duty and retired military.

[31] For a study of the military in the economy, see Gerard McCarthy, *Military Capitalism in Myanmar: Examining the Origins, Continuities and Evolution of "Khaki Capitalism"*, Trends in Southeast Asia, no. 6/2019 (Singapore: ISEAS – Yusof Ishak Institute, 2019).

Myanmar had become a pariah state in Western circles after 1988, as the US and EU imposed sanctions, and, effectively, Aung San Suu Kyi made US policy,[32] which called for regime change and recognition of the 1990 election results as politically legitimate. Although Japanese aid continued to be important, there was a clear movement towards China in terms of provision of military equipment and training. Both the Thein Sein government and the US Obama administration sought to ease confrontation, and this occurred with the release of multitudes of political prisoners and Aung San Suu Kyi from house arrest.[33] Perhaps the Tatmadaw under Thein Sein sought a degree of political legitimacy by improving its international standing on internal rights.

When Aung San Suu Kyi and the NLD stopped its boycotts of by-elections, and began to participate directly in the political process, Tatmadaw influence was partly disbursed, but its control over its core interests remained.

If, in 2015, Senior General Than Shwe[34] had been asked about how history would judge Tatmadaw rule, he might well have said: It was a great success: it held the country together, opened the economy, was nationalistic and supported Buddhism, emphasized the nation's military heritage, and promised a multi-party "discipline-flourishing democracy" and delivered on that pledge. Yet at the same time, the military remained in its proper role as guardian of the state and its defender while perpetuating state interests and ensuring that those of the Tatmadaw through the provisions of the 2008 constitution, would be maintained in any future government.

Internal and external observers would certainly dispute the imputed Than Shwe comments postulated above because of the costs to the people and the lack of alternative avenues of progress. Although the military have

---

[32] See David Steinberg, "Aung San Suu Kyi and U.S. Policy Toward Myanmar", *Journal of Current Southeast Asian Affairs*, September 2010.

[33] Council on Foreign Relations, "U.S. Policy Towards Burma: Issues for the 112th Congress", United States, 8 August 2011. https://www.everycrsreport.com/reports/R41971.html

[34] He retired as commander-in-chief in March 2011 with the formation of the new administration.

stipulated economic and social programmes as part of their objectives, they have not been of core concern. So, judging Myanmar history under military domination in terms of performance legitimacy and improvement in the lives of its inhabitants, the record has been one of failure. The public has tragically illustrated its frustrations on numerous occasions through violence in the streets: 1962 student unrest, demonstrations over U Thant's funeral (1974), the failed popular uprising of 1988, the "saffron revolution" of 2007, and in unmanipulated voting in the 1990, 2015, and 2020 elections (and by-elections as well), and now following the 1 February 2021 coup. Civilian Bamah fear of the military has been apparent and ubiquitous through most of the military domination period, while ethnic minority suspicions and resentment against the *Tatmadaw* are obvious in their continuing reliance on attempted armed autonomy. An adjectively modified ("discipline-flourishing") "democracy" indicates a questionable use of that designation in a modern, international context.

The abject failure of the military-backed USDP in the 2015 elections may have antagonized the Tatmadaw, but it did not threaten their core institutional interests, although it seems to affected personal leadership. Tatmadaw interests were:

- National unity and national sovereignty[35]
- Control over minority affairs
- Retention of all coercive power (police, intelligence, military)
- Control over its own military affairs
- Control to prevent change it does not want through constitutional provisions
- Prevention against charges brought against anyone in earlier military administrations who acted on official business ("get out of jail free" provision of the constitution)
- Explicit political role for military; "participation of the Tatmadaw in the leading role of national politics in the future"

---

[35] For a study of military ideology, see Ye Phone Kyaw, "The Development of National Ideology in Myanmar: Political Socialization and the Role of the Tatmadaw since the Second World War", *Journal of Burma Studies* 24, no. 2 (2020).

- Defending the constitution (of 2008)
- Internal stability—avoidance of "chaos"

This list clearly indicated that democracy is not a core interest of the Tatmadaw. Of the seventy-two years of independent Burma/Myanmar, the Tatmadaw has ruled directly by decree over thirty-seven years (1958–60, 1962–74, 1988–2011, 2021–?), through constitutions it formulated over nineteen years (1974–88, 2011–16), and with stipulated controls over five years (2016–21), with only twelve years of civilian administration, although with a strong military role.

As Tatmadaw control continued, the military grew: from about 110,000 in 1958, to 140,000 in 1965, to 200,000 in 1988, and then to about 400,000 in 1999. The goal was said to be 500,000. There were in addition some 80,000 police under Tatmadaw control. The graduating class at the Defence Services Academy grew from 127 in 1989 to 2,440 in 2009. Virtually all in the senior Tatmadaw leadership were Burman and Buddhist. Officers were also recruited through the ranks in an officer corps training institution that had less prestige than the Academy.[36]

The military budget in 2014 was US$2.4 billion, or 14 per cent of government expenditures, and in 2013 it was 4.5 per cent of GDP, the highest in Southeast Asia.[37] Expenditures are likely to continue to be high as the military requires more sophisticated equipment and high maintenance costs. Off-budget expenses are unknown but likely to be extensive.

---

[36] See Nakanishi, *Strong Soldiers, Failed Revolution.* In 1917–18, the military budget was 14.1 per cent of the Union government expenditures. Maung Aung Myoe, "The Defence Expenditures and Commercial Interests of the Tatmadaw", in *Praetorians, Profiteers or Professionals? Studies on the Militaries of Myanmar and Thailand.* edited by Michael J. Montesano, Terence Chong, and Prajak Kongkirati (Singapore: ISEAS – Yusof Ishak Institute, 2020), p. 103

[37] Robert H. Taylor, *The Armed Forces in Myanmar: A Terminating Role?*, Trends in Southeast Asia, no. 2/2015 (Singapore: Institute of Southeast Asian Studies, 2015).

THE LONGEVITY OF MILITARY INFLUENCE

What factors in this long history of the Tatmadaw's domination of the state of Burma/Myanmar contributed to this domination, and are likely to influence its future role? These have been multiple, complex, and varied over time.

The cohesion of the senior Tatmadaw officers has been an essential element of its longevity, and recognized as such by the state, for the most heinous crime under the junta (with which Aung San Suu Kyi was accused) was attempting to split the military. Ne Win probably held the military together in the face of ideological disagreements. After Ne Win, apparently the senior active-duty officers in the Tatmadaw knew it must remain united to preserve its perquisites and authority.[38] This was evident in the September 1988 coup, and illustrated when in October 2004 Senior General Than Shwe fired and jailed General Khin Nyunt (head of Military Intelligence, Prime Minister, and Secretary-1 of the SPDC) and most of Khin Nyunt's entourage, and almost immediately went on a state visit to India without fear of reprisals. "In Burma, the cohesion of the Tatmadaw has never faced a decisive crisis, and even when the Ne Win regime collapsed, and even though the military regime has continued so long."[39]

Aung San was the single Burmese who had Weberian charismatic authority, an aura built up over time and fostered by his daughter (controversial statues were erected of him in minority regions under Aung San Suu Kyi's reign and over local ethnic objections). Ne Win had authority, despite serious mistakes, but no cult of the personality, which now seems evident for Aung San Suu Kyi.[40] The Tatmadaw's admiration for its leader was strongest for Ne Win because of his historic role and control of military promotions and civilian placements. Still, Than Shwe

---

[38] Guardian Sein Win. Personal communication.

[39] Nakanishi, *Strong Soldiers, Failed Revolution*, 285.

[40] Burmese concepts of power are often divided into two: *ana* and *awza*. *Ana* is coercive power, which the military has, but moral authority is *awza*, and has resided in Aung San Suu Kyi.

was respected because of his reform programme and modernization efforts. General Saw Maung did not seem to command such respect during his short term as head of the SLORC, perhaps because of his unstable mental condition.[41] The early unquestioned leadership of Aung San and Ne Win perhaps cemented the importance of those roles.

With personalized leadership and entourage formation, corruption became the oil that greased relationships. The early military authorities were not corrupt, but the continuation of power in their hands changed the pattern.

The absence of effective civilian leadership was a contributing factor. Of course, the Tatmadaw did what it could to prevent the rise of alternative sources of influence or power. To date there seems no concerted effort in the NLD to train a new generation of leaders within the civilian community to replace the aging leadership, which in turn may not understand the attitudes and emotions of the Z generation.

In contrast to all other military regimes in Asia, the Tatmadaw has been the only government that has completely been able to control social mobility. No one could rise in society without military approval, and the military channel was at first desirable, then useful for even families opposed to military rule, and now as generational military families become common. A single-party system controlled by the Tatmadaw prevented unauthorized access through politics. Socialism cut off economic advancement. Education was contained and monitored, as were the elements of advocacy civil society. Information, entry and exit were all under military command.[42] Even the hierarchy of the *sangha* and its educational institutions were tightly controlled. The breadth and intensity of control were unique in Asia. This only began to be modified under the Thein Sein administration beginning in 2010.

---

[41] He is said to have remarked to Western journalists about handing power to the NLD should it win the 1990 elections. This would have been anathema to many Tatmadaw leaders.

[42] See David I. Steinberg, "The Persistence of Military Dominance", *Myanmar: The Dynamics of an Evolving Polity*, edited by Steinberg (Boulder, CO: Lynne Rienner, 2015), Ch 3.

Political legitimacy[43] in any state must constantly be reaffirmed through actions, attitudes and policies. It is never static. In the early period of Burmese independence, this legitimacy was built into the actions and myths of its early leadership and its role in the search for independence and then in protecting the state. Leadership could not be challenged on these accounts.[44] Attempts to transfer legitimacy to surviving family members of deceased leaders have been apparent in Burma, Indonesia, the Philippines, South Korea, Bangladesh, and Pakistan.

The defence of Buddhism became a singular aspect of the search for legitimacy of all Burmese governments, starting with U Nu. As one official proclaimed, "To be Burmese is to be Buddhist." Although Ne Win was never, earlier in his career, known as a particularly devout Buddhist, as he aged, he built his own pagoda, and the official media consistently stressed his devotion to Buddhism. During the period of the junta, this was even more pronounced with the renovations on the Shwedagon in Yangon, the new pagoda only a few feet shorter in Naypyidaw, and repairs in the ancient capital of Bagan.[45] Others were built by the leadership as well. The myth and illusion that Muslims were out to destroy Buddhism in Myanmar became an element in the official and social media and reinforced the Buddhist legitimacy approach. Anti-Muslim, and especially anti-Rohingya, sentiment has been prominent in state-sponsored media and propaganda.[46]

---

[43] For a study of political legitimacy in Myanmar, see David I. Steinberg, *Turmoil in Burma: Contested Legitimacies in Myanmar* (Norwalk: EastBridge, 2006). See also Steinberg, "Legitimacy in Burma: Concepts and Implications", in *Myanmar: State, Society, and Ethnicity*, edited by N. Ganesan and Kyaw Yin Hlaing (Singapore: Hiroshima Peace Institute and Institute of Southeast Asian Studies, 2007).

[44] This is in marked contrast to South Korea, where Park Chung Hee had no national legitimacy—he was an officer in the Japanese colonial army, and the last successful coup in Korea was in 1392. His search for legitimacy was in economic development.

[45] Aung San Suu Kyi is said to be building a pagoda in Naypyidaw as well.

[46] Immediately following the February 2021 coup, the official media was full of reaffirming Buddhist activities, obviously designed to provide legitimacy to the military actions.

The Tatmadaw has built up a renewed emphasis on the military in Burmese history. It erected statues of militarily successful kings, and rebuilt the royal palaces in Mandalay, Pegu, and Shwebo in questionably authentic style. Textbooks were rewritten and pseudo-scientific studies spread indicating the early origins of man and civilization in Myanmar (North Korea attempted similar propaganda). Aung San was claimed to be the fourth great unifier of the country, and Ne Win was touted as the great solidifier. Displays at the National Museum and the Defence Services Museum reinforce these positions.

The political need to get the economy out of foreign hands (British, Indian or Chinese) was also an important element of legitimacy, resulting in the emphasis on socialism, although with earlier precedent as royal control existed over foreign trade, the teak forests and oil extraction, which were royal monopolies in the pre-colonial era. This was reinforced by a xenophobic concern about foreigners in general, and the susceptibility of Burmese women to foreign blandishments (and that Aung San Suu Kyi had married a British academic, and Muslim men marrying Buddhist women, although the expressed fear is as early as Kipling's poem "The Road to Mandalay"). This, of course, was a major impetus to the democratic socialism in the civilian period, and the later ideological rigidity on the military. It remains a muted but real concern over foreign investment. The suspended construction of the Chinese-sponsored Myitsone Dam in the Kachin State by President Thein Sein in 2011was in part a reaction against growing Chinese influence in society through public and private investments and illegal immigration.

The specific military emphasis on paternalism has been a popular appeal to the Burman population. "Only the army is mother. The army is father" were slogans on billboards in the 1990s,[47] while the military has chided people for revering their "aunt" (i.e., Aung San Suu Kyi) over their parents. The Tatmadaw had, in its own view, become *in loco parentis*. This was repeated in the media following the February 2021 coup.

---

[47] Callahan, *Making Enemies*, p. 207. See also Nakanishi, *Strong Soldiers, Failed Revolution*, p. 294.

The Tatmadaw has transformed the need for reversion of economic assets into Burmese hands into significant direct control over major economic interests. Dirigiste economic policies, obviously present in society, have reinforced military interests, first through the Union Solidarity and Development Association (later formed into a party) to the Myanmar Economic Holding Corporation,[48] and the Myanmar Economic Corporation, each employing tens of thousands of workers, some with a monopoly on sectors, and with significant foreign investment. The Office of Procurement of the Ministry of Defence is a further element of the Tatmadaw's economic interests, and the Directorate of Defence Industries controls factories providing civilian as well as military goods. All of these enable the military to supplement their allotted official budget at unaccountable levels. While the Indonesian and Thai military also hold economic assets, though less than before, the South Korean military did not have direct economic interests.

As the Tatmadaw opened society to private sector activities, its "cronies" (a word that became popular in the Philippines under Marcos)—those civilian and retired military with personal links to the military establishment—began to acquire assets, resulting in specialized opportunities to acquire wealth, and transforming Burmese society from one of shared poverty to one with growing income disparities. Standards for their contribution to Myanmar's development were lacking or never enforced.

The classic justification of military rule is the need to protect the state. In Myanmar, the protection stems essentially from internal enemies, although some, like the Burma Communist Party, were blatantly supported by the Chinese Communist Party. Fear of a US invasion, and the paramilitary training of some men to stave off an American attack, was an example of paranoia but served to strengthen the Tatmadaw's internal

---

[48] An auditor of the Myanmar Economic Holding Corporation indicated that the corporation never calculated the use of government personnel or facilities in its estimates of profits and losses, so it would never lose money. But individual personnel and units could invest in the corporation to supplement personal or institutional incomes.

resolve, if not the public's understanding.[49] Whether the movement of the capital from Yangon to Naypyidaw in 2005 was in part a result of this fear (royal Burmese regimes had often moved their capitals for strategic or occult reasons) is uncertain, but the movement of the air command from Mingaladon (a Yangon suburb) to Meiktila in central Myanmar, and the naval command from Sittwe on the coast in Rakhine State to Ann, inland in the same state, is evidence of this concern.

The constitution calls for a single Tatmadaw; the dilemma is how to incorporate the rebellious ethnic forces from diverse groups, the total number of such troops being estimated at over 50,000. The attempt by the government to emasculate them by proposing their incorporation as border guard forces with essentially Burman control was ineffective except for some very minor groups. The issue remains unresolved, and the Tatmadaw does not have the power to defeat the major ethnic rebellions along the state's diverse periphery. Since one provision for a return to civilian rule after the February 2021 coup is to make all efforts to bring "eternal peace" to the region, this is a most questionable, unlikely determinant.

Aside from the "commonsensical" (as Aung San Suu Kyi noted) need for Myanmar to remain friendly with China, China's backing of state and military action considering the Rohingya tragedy strengthened its position. Improved relations with India and Thailand, Japan's continuing support, and Myanmar's entry into ASEAN in 1997 under military auspices all increased Myanmar's role and Tatmadaw legitimacy. Aung San Suu Kyi may have been foreign minister, but her performance, especially at the International Court of Justice in defence of the Tatmadaw's atrocities against the Rohingya, was obviously designed to placate military concerns and to enhance her political standing in the forthcoming elections of 2020 (it probably helped her); it had the reverse effect abroad.

---

[49] A Military Intelligence colonel believed that the United States would invade Myanmar; holding up the fingers on his hands said, "Granada, Panama, Somalia, Kosovo, Afghanistan, Iraq." Personal communication.

The approximately seventeen years that the Tatmadaw took to write its constitution, finally promulgated in a manipulated referendum during the cyclone of 2008, was simply to delay the onset of the document that it had carefully scripted. Its provisions ensure that if there is military unity, no changes can occur that will threaten the enhanced position it has imposed on society. Although Aung San Suu Kyi and foreign observers generally focus on the provision that prevents her from becoming president or vice president, the important provisions related to the continuity of military control prevent amendments (the military have 25 per cent of all seats at parliamentary national and subnational levels) and control over three critical ministries (Defence, Home Affairs, Border Affairs), a majority on the National Defence and Security Council, and an explicit provision for the Tatmadaw's role in the political affairs of state.[50] Although Senior General Than Shwe may have conceived of the USDP as playing a controlling role, this has been demonstrated both in the 2015 and 2020 elections to be an illusion, but constitutional provisions and the defence of that document remain core to Tatmadaw interests.

The revolutions in the streets of the "Arab Spring" states may have sobered the Tatmadaw to the need to partly unclench their fist over the society. The failed people's revolution of 1988 resulted in the coup of September 1988, and the suppressed "saffron revolution" of monks in 2007 may have speeded up the process of constitution formation in 2008 that had been lackadaisically under way since about 1991. Whether prompted by internal considerations or to assuage foreign elements that change was possible, or both, is impossible to now determine, but the necessity for change was apparent at the top. Awaiting another popular outbreak that might split the military and succeed was not deemed an option. So reform came from the leadership; the only other place in Asia where this happened was in Taiwan.

But reform was not necessarily an indication of a democratic process, but rather of a multi-party political system with constraints. "It would be

---

[50] The model was *dwi fungsi* (dual military and civilian functions) of Indonesia in the post-Sukarno period.

more accurate to view Myanmar's transition in 2010 less as a transition to democracy than to a diarchy with competing forms of government."[51]

THE COUP OF 1 FEBRUARY 2021: INSTITUTIONAL AND EMOTIVE CONTRASTS

From a Tatmadaw vantage point, then, by all objective and institutional measures, the perpetuation of military control over their perceived interests had been achieved. Their protection was assured even though the NLD had won an even larger win in the National Parliament than had been anticipated by most observers, taking 396 of the available 426 seats in the 8 November elections. The USDP won only seven seats in the upper house, twenty-six in the lower house, and only thirty-eight in all the state/regional parliaments—far less than expected and in vast contrast to its extensive Naypyidaw physical headquarters, built to endorse materially its projected (but unrealized) role in state affairs. It was, in essence, a disgraceful, humiliating result in contrast to what the military had hoped or planned. The Parliament was due to assemble on 1 February to form the new government to be installed on 1 April (also the start of the Burmese fiscal year). Yet the Tatmadaw maintained its veto over constitutional amendments and was protected.

If, indeed, the military retained control over its core interests through constitutional means that could not be overturned by the NLD, which seemed to have been the case, and recognized its own continuing authority, then a coup or military takeover would seem unnecessary despite the election results. What were the basic causes of the coup, as contrasted with the ostensible voting fraud charges that were denied by election observers? Was, thus, the coup unnecessary from the Tatmadaw's institutional position?

Speculation is rife. Did the military misperceive the extent of its own power? The latter seems unlikely. Did the Tatmadaw leadership

---

[51] Ingrid Jordt, Tharaphi Than and Sue Ye Lin, *How Generation Z Galvanized a Revolutionary Movement against Myanmar's 2021 Military Coup*, Trends in Southeast Asia, no. 7/2021 (Singapore: ISEAS – Yusof Ishak Institute, 2021), p. 3.

anticipate splits in its ranks that could have undercut its monopoly on its power and role? This is also unclear. Some claim that the Tatmadaw actually expected a victory because of the maladministration of the NLD, and their lack of understanding of popular attitudes. Others were disappointed that retired militarymen were not brought into the NLD administration and/or elected from local constituencies. If the USDP had done better, and minor Bamah and ethnic parties won a significant number of seats, then with a 25 per cent active-duty military, a Tatmadaw backed government might have been formed, and Senior General Min Aung Hlaing might have been president.

The collapse of the USDP denies the Senior General a personal political/constitutional route to presidential power, for even if he were nominated to become one of the two vice presidents (one of the two will be from the Tatmadaw), that role has far less influence than his present one. It seems unlikely he would want that position, and the coup at least clarified the extent of his political ambitions.

In the month after his coup, Min Aung Hlaing followed many of the same strategies used in earlier military coups. The military arrested key political leaders and engaged in tactics intended to divide the remaining political opposition—for example, by inviting other political parties disaffected by the NLD into the new SAC government. It paid obeisance to the head of the State Sangha Council or *Ma-ha-na*, and it performed *yadaya* rituals to combat bad *karma*. It arrested *bedin saya*—soothsayers or astrologers—who challenged Min Aung Hlaing's dark rituals with counter spells. The military also sought to justify its *coup d'état* to international audiences by, in this instance, using democratic claims. And it sowed chaos and violence in Myanmar's cities to demonstrate that the junta alone could protect society from anarchists and rabble rousers. At the core of these strategies was a broader argument justifying autocratic rule: that only the military could protect the unity of the Buddhist Bamar nation and that Min Aung Hlaing was the apotheosis of society and the state.[52]

---

[52] Ibid., pp. 6–7.

Thus, the basic reasons for the coup and the formation of the State Administration Council, as the Tatmadaw government wishes to be known, as opposed to the publicly articulated charges of voter fraud, remain opaque and are, perhaps, personal. Although this coup may have been in the planning stages for days or even longer following the 8 November elections, observers have noted that by the day before the coup, all of the regional military commanders had agreed to it. Some observers believe that an analysis of Min Aung Hlaing's previous actions over more than a year indicate that he was following a pattern that anticipated a route to supreme power in the state. This may thus have been more a personal affirmation of power than an institutional one, with the anticipated acquiescence of the Tatmadaw leadership, who would also gain or sustain its perquisites.

Two factors may have been important determinants of this action. The first is the personal antipathy between Min Aung Hlaing and Aung San Suu Kyi, who had not personally met for a long period.[53] This distrust is increasingly important in a society in which personalized power has been an essential attribute of governance since the beginnings of the Burmese kingdoms. As one observer remarked, Aung San Suu Kyi confronted the Tatmadaw head on when she should have attempted or established some reasonable relationship and nibbled away at its flanks of power. This was a tactical error of great importance. Perhaps because of her own self-esteem as Aung San's daughter, she has not been an

---

[53] Some observers speculate that the coup was because Min Aung Hlaing was supposed to retire this year at age 65 (in 2014 the retirement age for the military was extended to 65 from 60), but the Tatmadaw is autonomous and could have extended his term without civilian consent. Others claim he was afraid of losing control over his and his family's personal economic assets. Some say that perhaps the NLD wanted publicly to dismantle the Tatmadaw's control over their obvious economic assets, but this appeared to be unlikely to occur, although questions over its off-budget enterprises and investments remain. What should not be disregarded is the internal self-image of militarymen as patriots and their actions as supportive of state interests, even when they are misguided. Some believe Aung San Suu Kyi refused to allow Min Aung Hlaing to become president, and refused to meet with him, thus providing a precipitating factor in the coup.

effective politician—a role she has personally described. This attitude of provocation is illustrated by the NLD concentrating on trying to change the provisions for the presidency, which denied her that role, and the extra-legal establishment of the role of state counsellor, which she held and said was above that of the presidency.[54] Arrogance on both sides of the tenuous power equation seems a complicating element in resolving the political issues facing the state. The NLD has participated in that arrogance, as has the Tatmadaw.

The second factor may have been emotional. The Tatmadaw have viewed themselves as the essential patriots and decried the Western advice to become a "regular" military, which they regard as essentially mercenary. They have considered themselves above that role. But they have been ridiculed extensively, and this has spread throughout the general population through social media, which is now ubiquitous (and which the military tried to limit or shut down immediately following the coup). This strikes a most painful wound. Where comedians had been jailed under the junta for sneering at the military, their influence could not readily be spread with internal censorship prevailing. The exceedingly poor political performance of the USDP in 2020 elections was said to have humiliated the Tatmadaw. This may seem to outsiders as a weak reason for such an important act, but it should not be dismissed. That the people (the Bamah majority) demeaned the military was insufferable. *Amour-propre* seems to have permeated both extremes of the political balance.

Aung San Suu Kyi and the civilian president were both put under house arrest, where they remain at this writing, and then charged with minor, manufactured "illegal" acts, and then she was charged with corruption and treason. Other civilian parliamentarians were arrested, released, and ordered home. The extent of the Tatmadaw's other arrests,

---

[54] It is worth noting that the president appointed after the February 2021 coup, General Myint Swe, had been nominated for that post in 2011, but withdrawn because his child had married a foreigner. They since divorced. The office of state counsellor was abolished by the Tatmadaw after the 1 February coup.

said to include over three thousand, and penetration into civil society, including the partial shutdown of the internet and control of cyber activities and some social media and press, is still evolving at this writing and is unclear. Previous laws limiting searches and seizures have been suspended for unspecified periods. Civil rights have markedly diminished for an unknown period.

At first, the Tatmadaw seemed to have learned lessons from the grim, lethal repression of mass demonstrations in 1988. Police were in the front lines, not the military, and lethal force less used. But this changed as the mass demonstrations continued and spread throughout the country. The Tatmadaw increasingly resorted to brute force to suppress them, so far without success. Over 700 people have said to have been killed in the violence at this writing. In a sense, the Tatmadaw has once again created the conditions for the "chaos" it deems necessary to control by instituting "law and order."

The Tatmadaw is, however, confronting a young generation that is significantly different from those who experienced the earlier coups and military regimes. The young "Z" generation, as they have been called, have grown up in an atmosphere of increasing freedom and are in touch with the world, and with each other, through technologies that are as ubiquitous as they are instant and open. This creates conditions that the Tatmadaw leadership—older and often isolated in Naypyidaw—clearly did not anticipate and which it seemingly cannot control without extreme violence, which simply increases the intensity of the opposition. A major percentage of the population is in this group, and the new technology has prevented the former isolation of the rural areas from urban trends. This young group, as with many worldwide incipient revolutionaries, has less to lose and are more prone to action.

Reverting to a pattern following the ignored 1990 elections, some elected NLD members formed a Committee Representing the Pyidaungsu Hluttaw (CRPH) claiming legitimacy, and went into hiding, while the Tatmadaw declared them treasonous and all those associated with it. The CRPH declared the 2008 constitution void, and was determined to form some sort of federal government, thus appealing to many ethnic minority interests. The CRPH seeks foreign recognition as the legitimate government of the state.

Civil disobedience organizations at the local level often took leadership roles in individual cases, and through technology could communicate instantly and spontaneously with other civil society organizations. But as suppression increased, so too has the non-violent civil movement entered into new and more dangerous phases.

The coup is destructive of the considerable progress in rights made over the past decade. This retrogression is likely to have profound effects on society for years. The Tatmadaw will probably play up the many ineffective attributes of NLD rule over the past five years, but this will not placate the people. The brutality of military suppression will long be remembered to the detriment of its own concepts of efficacy and patriotism.

The Tatmadaw has promised to return the government to civilian rule after one year if various conditions are met. The same promise was made in 1958 after the "constitutional coup", and the military supervised a relatively free election in 1960 in which their preferred party lost. This time it may be far more difficult.[55] These conditions are:

- Reforming the voting lists;
- Reconstituting of the Election Commission;
- Preventing the continuing COVID-19 outbreak;
- Helping businesses recover as quickly as possible; and
- "Efforts will be placed as much as possible on restoring eternal peace all over the country to accord with the National Ceasefire Agreement (NCA)."
- "When these tasks have been completed to accord with the State of Emergency, a free and fair multi-party election will be held, and then, the assigned duty of the state will be handed over to the winning party meeting norms and standards of democracy."[56]

---

[55] Office of the Commander-in-Chief of Defence Services, Republic of the Union of Myanmar, Notification No. 1/2021, 1 February 2021. https://www.gnlm.com.mm/republic-of-the-union-of-myanmar-office-of-the-commander-in-chief-of-defence-services-notification-no-1-2021/

[56] "Notification No. 1, 1 February 2021, Office of the Commander-in-Chief of Defence Services", *Global New Light of Myanmar* [Naypyidaw], 2 February 2021.

Attainment of some of the provisions is questionable; "eternal peace", has not existed since independence. What is evident, even before the fourth coup, was that the Tatmadaw would continue to be an essential influence in that society. This coup simply reinforces that conclusion in dire terms. The Tatmadaw has forbidden the use of the terms "junta" and "regime", to emphasize their transient intentions, referring to itself as the State Administration Council.

International reactions—those strong in condemnation—are mixed in action. The United States has imposed further, mostly personalized sanctions, frozen Myanmar assets in the United States, and stopped official developmental assistance to the government (not humanitarian aid to NGOs), but with minimal effect. Min Aung Hlaing is already under personalized sanctions because of the Rohingya ethnic cleansing and human rights violations. The EU has followed suit, but Asia will likely not do so. China, Japan, India, South Korea and all of ASEAN will probably abstain. Chinese officials will support any stable Myanmar government, and have characterized the coup as simply a significant cabinet change,[57] although their tone has changed after Chinese enterprises were torched in an industrial zone.

How might this dilemma be resolved? Some have suggested that the Tatmadaw might agree to change the constitution to a proportional voting system under new elections, which would give the USDP more seats (some respectable number but not a majority), and increased authority for some minorities, which had become disillusioned with NLD attitudes towards them. This would fragment non-Tatmadaw power. Whether this would satisfy critics is questionable. Whether the NLD would agree is unlikely. At this stage, there seems no compromise position acceptable to either party.

---

[57] Under pressure from the United States. in the 1990s to sanction Myanmar, Japan stopped official assistance but continued humanitarian aid, but redefined that term to include infrastructure such as the Yangon airport and rehabilitation of the Beluchaung hydroelectric dam.

SUMMATION

There are no indications in Myanmar that the military will intentionally in the longer or shorter term play any less decisive role than in the past. But gradual attrition of military domination through liberalizations already in place, now set back by the coup, is likely to be slowed over time.[58] Yet, "What we are seeing is not just a contest between authoritarianism and democracy, which it also is, but a contest between two distinct ideas of sovereignty, one based on the will of the people and the other based on the idea of karmic kingship."[59]

Is some form of quicker change possible? An egregiously unacceptable incident could split the military leadership, allowing constitutional changes. This would require a transformation in military attitudes and alleviation of suspicions towards a civilian administration. If the military or elements thereof refuse to fire on civilians in widespread demonstrations, this could force reforms. These seem unlikely at this writing.

The most important aspects of the complex set of factors that have allowed the military to continue in power are both positive and negative. The control of all coercive forces within the state has been essential, but so has its unity and the unique control over all aspects of social mobility and change (until after 2010). No foreign power or element has exerted sufficient pressure (if that were possible, which is highly unlikely) on the Tatmadaw to relinquish authority, no matter how foreign regimes might have disliked that government. In many instances, an autocratic state with a strong command structure is easier to deal with than a vibrant democracy with multiples of conflicting interests. A state, as in the past, in which its peripheries are open to foreign exploitation of peoples and materials offers opportunities that might not occur under a representative power structure.

---

[58] One cabinet official, an astute retired officer, told the author that the amalgam of civilians and military in the parliament will be the "end game" in military rule, as the officers will learn to respect civilians and gradually give up power.

[59] Jordt, "Notes on the Coup in Myanmar: Karmic Kingship, Legitimacy, and Sovereignty".

It was not only the West that took no definitive action, as about 2008 when the Tatmadaw thought an invasion might happen because of US regime change policies, but earlier in the BSPP era the Chinese and the Soviets did not believe that Burma was really socialist—rather state capitalist, and China supported the Burma Communist Party. The unity of the autocratic state, however abhorrent to observers, was more important than democratic chaos if brought about through foreign intervention.

Restoring the status quo ante before the coup is impossible. Should the Tatmadaw prevail in the near term, it would solve nothing over the longer period, for it would be in their perceived. interests to tighten their control over society, which in turn would increase various forms of civil resistance that would likely burst forth over some event. So too, if the CRPH were to assume any modicum of power, they would try to form a new constitution limiting Tatmadaw authority and perhaps increasing the modest autonomy of the ethnic minorities. They have already publicly discarded the constitution of 2008. The CRPH has asked for recognition by foreign governments of its role as the legitimate state authority.

Western governments, the media, and observers as a general principle deplore military rule. Yet, as Selth noted, "The Tatmadaw is likely to remain the most powerful political institution in Myanmar."[60] Western societies are likely to be frustrated by delayed, uneven, and jiggered progress, and prefer relatively quick reforms, often invoking with the media the imagined "road towards democracy," however defined. This is a simplistic concept of change, and contrary to modern experience.[61] If there is regression on this supposed road, they sometimes impose sanctions.[62] But positive change in Myanmar is likely to be slow, and shrouded in nationalistic rhetoric—two steps backward, one step

---

[60] Andrew Selth, "Strong, Fully Efficient and Modern: Myanmar's New Look Armed Forces", Regional Outlook Paper 49, Griffith Asia Institute, 2016, p. 1.

[61] See Aurel Croissant, "Transforming Civil-Military Relations: Myanmar in Comparative Perspective", Stimson Center, Washington, DC, April 2021.

[62] The first question to be asked when imposing any regimen of sanctions is: what are the realistic conditions under which these sanctions could be waived? This is rarely asked.

forward, to paraphrase and reverse Lenin. And, as they say, *bamah-lo*—
in the Burmese manner, and still strongly influenced by military interests.
The fourth coup is an example of this unfortunate tendency.

After the fourth coup, one might well be reminded of the salient
and prescient remark in the 1990s by Col. Kyi Maung on the role of the
military in Myanmar: "The play is over, but the audience is forced to
remain in their seats, and the actors refuse to leave the stage."[63]

---

[63] Personal communication. Kyi Maung was a member of the Revolutionary
Council in 1958, then head of the Southern Command, jailed by Ne Win under
the BSPP, and was Aung San Suu Kyi's spokesman until they had a falling out.